Contents

Chekhov's Mongoose

TOM SHAPCOTT (born 1935) is a well known Australian poet who has been published in a number of countries. Translations of major selections of his work have been published in Hungary, Romania and the Republic of Macedonia. He has published 15 collections of poems in Australia, as well as 6 novels and other prose works. He is the inaugural Professor of Creative Writing at the University of Adelaide, in South Australia.

Chekhov's Mongoose

Tom Shapcott

SALT

PUBLISHED BY SALT PUBLISHING
PO Box 202, Applecross, Western Australia 6153
PO Box 937, Great Wilbraham, Cambridge PDO CB1 5JX United Kingdom

© Tom Shapcott, 2000

The right of Tom Shapcott to be identified as the
author of this work has been asserted by him in accordance
with Section 77 of the Copyright, Designs and Patents Act 1988.

First published 2000

Printed and bound in the United States of America by Lightning Source

Typeset in Swift 9.5 / 13

British Library Cataloguing-in-Publication Data
A catalogue record for this book is available from the British Library

National Library of Australia
Cataloguing-in-publication data

Shapcott, Thomas W. (Thomas William), 1935–.
Chekhov's mongoose.

ISBN 0 646 39543 2

I. Title.

A821.3

SP

1 3 5 7 9 8 6 4 2

To Bruce and Brenda Beaver

Acknowledgments

Acknowledgements are due to the editors of the following publications in which some of the poems in this collection first appeared: *The Age, Antipodes, The Australian, The Australian's Review of Books, The Bunyip, Canberra Times, Eureka Street, Heat, Imago, Meanjin, Mind the Gap* (New York), *Overland, Poetry Review, Poetryetc* (internet), *Quadrant, Sidewalk, Southerly, Westerly.*

I   The Dreams

The old window

His architect had played the post-modern game—
allusions everywhere but never serious,
illusions short-sheeted, as in the classic maze
(one-quarter size) that set off the Rotunda
(pure Raj, that) where the outdoor drinks'
casquet was the Party Piece. That first summer
he used the Orangerie the once,
for the Corporate Retreat (the name fooled nobody);
it was a pure assertion of his trendy nonchelance.
Later he hired out the space for wedding groups
(his maze was trampled by Mediterranean types).
The ground floor area also was public as an Insurance lobby
or the Piazza of one of the Accountancy agglomerates.
The Grand Staircase, a cheeky salute to the TITANIC,
invited theatrical gestures, and it got them.
Nobody would forget Amanda abandoning her seven veils
as she ascended to the upstairs bathroom
and her nip of Mother's Downfall. Or Geneviève
breasting the bannister in the altogether
too dégagé mink stole.
                              He had his parties,
everyone remembered. It was a fun place,
Raoul's Verseilles.
                              There was an attic
or at least a Mansard roof and small rooms.
Each window was different (that was the trick)
and he had insisted to the architect
that the furthest window must be the genuine thing,
a tiny multi-paned dormer ripped
from the chateau his grandmother once haunted
outside Lyons. It was only in the wettest day of winter
that he finally clambered up and regarded the memento.
Perhaps it had been enough to know it was there.
He had looked at it in Australia once before, out of storage,
and the slap of antipodean light, brash as an appraising squint
over the tanned bodies in Bondi out to the glittering surf
had reduced that sheltered window frame to an imperfect excuse

for clumsy glass and bubbly surfaces (which he once remembered
as meaningful). He saw through it, it might be said.

But in winter glumness, with drops clustering
like dismal starlings on the outer panes, he re-entered its world.
He had not escaped her after all.
His mother still trembled for him, and remained as powerless.
His father slammed the door again and the same pane cracked.
His grandmother was as imperious and demanded her price.
And he was the still-young boy again. "Mon petit serviteur",
she had said, again and again. "Serviteur"
as she instructed him, cruelly, in all the arts.
The Mansard attic was his choice. Even then
he only had to raise one finger and he knew she was lost.
So he came home to this, because loss is power
and power is lost, and because illusion
can be allusion, after all, in the end.

An old story

Twenty-three years later he sat on his bed
in the dark in the same room.
Like irridescent dust, his hair
now covered his body—shoulder,
belly, and of course the luxuriant beard.
Only his skull was hairless, nothing
would alter that. For twenty-one
of those years he had looked at each mirror
and always the verdict: going going gone.
There was the cheval-glass
in Madame Véronique's salon—she
called it a salon—and the gold framed
Verseilles monstrosity of his ambassadorial days,
that had been an indulgence. More important
was the small steel mirror—army issue—
it was still close to hand, had he needed it.
Like a blue army in the green heat
it had multiplied in his mind over the years
and always with the same curse:
twenty-three years will pass, and you will be
back to where you started.
Slowly he got up off the bed.
He reached for his razor.

Phoenix

The Phoenix was not where I thought it should be—
perched, say, on the rim of the volcano
warming its eggs like the Galapagos shag.
I had to be more brazen, for instance,
and insist I had more than mere information.
I had to flaunt everything like (to make a parallel)
some Mandril or one of the more conspicuous monkeys.

And not only that, there was the matter of etiquette:
if you thought the mating rituals of bowerbirds and the Huon
    Pine
were overdone—all display and little return—
what could have possibly prepared you for this?
Or prepared me? I was the guineapig,
or the sacrificial lamb, or the shearer's dog.
Place yourself in my position:
I have travelled light, I have had the right vaccinations
and the best Skin Shields and my mobile
is state of the art
except that it might as well have been State of the Ark.

In these conditions, the Phoenix was,
as the saying is, risen. No gender games here.
Merely self expression. That was the rub.
Who can bargain with volcanoes?
How was I to know the Phoenix
was my own past come back to haunt?
What I tried to take was already taken.

Aubade

They were not young. Age had wrinkled
and crumpled those parts of the body that crumple,
it had narrowed their vision into a tunnel
where things at the edges are an effort
and are always somehow disturbing,
like a dogfight in a neighbouring yard
or noises that could be a branch cracking
or a fencepost (why?) thrown out of joint.
They had entered the time of other things
somehow happening elsewhere, of half-heard
exclamations and shouts and whispers.
They had become alone, even between themselves.
He would make coffee and call to her
expecting an answer though he knew her answer
was always yes. She would murmur
and protest at his clothes strewn over the bathroom floor
though had it ever been otherwise? They would get up
in the morning together, in the same order,
but as always there would be the moment, too,
when they would meet with a certain surprise,
out in the garden, she with a mattock in her hand
he dragging out the hose. They would pause, then,
and reach out, as if it were the first time,
touching each other with the very tips of their fingers.

Deposition of the dream

Why are dreams always so cruel?
Even in telling them, and laughing,
freshening them up so as to fool
the shiver out of them, we are saving
some part for our own torment, later.

"I had this dream"—and at once we back
away, if we are listeners. We've been caught
before, and not by you, or our own lack
of preparedness. You do not have to be taught
to flinch, it arrives sooner before later.

I had this dream and it was not cruel,
it was beautiful. The dream was of love
and protection, of us as we once were, full
of our very first sharing. Dove. Dove.
You get the glint in it? The knife comes later.

In my dream, she was worn and alone
and she clung to me (as she once had to cling)
so that I closed her eyes with kisses. Not one
sob went uncomforted. My arms were strong
as if this had been their condition forever.

Did those people die? Did they recover?
The deposition, once lodged, keeps the matter
open. Even to laugh is to finger
such dusty files you must sneeze, or utter
denials, complicity, a further

complication. Why do old deceptions return?
Is it true: to stay silent is better?
Life is not dry, it is no deposition.
Dreams are the comfort of sucking what's bitter.
Once lodged, dream evidence files you forever.

The letters

"Dear Mater and Dad" he had written. Or
to his brother, "Old Salt, how goes it back home?"
He wrote with a blunt pencil by candle-light
or in the Red Shield Hut well away from the Front.
He tried not to get mud on the small pages, or fingerprints,
or blood. He invented memories of Leave in the Old Dart
full of meals eaten and jolly girls or sometimes the Cinema
or that time in the Gods trying to hear a play
(it was a Comedy but he missed so much). Three times
that particular night returned but he never got it right—
the damp and cold through his feet, the smell of steaming wool,
the girl herself twisting her two hands ceaselessly—
not once did his letters reinvent how it was,
or even how he wished it to be. In the front line, though,
what was important was the act of writing,
of getting it down. 'It' was the affirmation
in his head, the thing clung to, the action
of language reduced to sign, as if signs
were a certain recipe for memory and wisdom.
None of the others in his tiny Signallers' group
wrote letters home. "Writing to yer Maw agen?"
Once he got it down and sealed it off
it went on a long journey that would alter everything.

When he finally got home, after the War,
his Mater was grim-faced with cancer, his Dad old
and that Old Salt his brother married and gone
without even a whiff of the mustard smell of his own War
which he couldn't write about. He couldn't accuse.
Well, that was all right.
                              Before she died
his Mater handed him the large bundle of letters.
"They kept her alive", his father said, it was the only time
he mentioned her agony years. Alone, in his childhood sleep-out
he opened the first one. It was another person, a child,
and he saw through the lies and was ashamed.
"Those letters proved to us that you still cared"

the Old Man said. "Though each one was a report from the dead
but we couldn't admit that. They took so long,
and so much could have happened. We read them
again and again." And for the first time he saw
how the lies and the cheerful reports hid nothing.
He was filled with agony. And it was for himself.

The old king after surgery

The years of anger now become months of claim.
Hunger as savage as he has ever known
demands this much: that he is not alone
in his private appetite but its private name
creates a public commodity. He called it 'shame'
but he was very wrong. He sought to disown
impulse and sexual greed, but it has grown
fiercer. All his oxygen burns in its flame.

And time's running out. He cannot afford pity
or modesty or doubt or compromise.
He was ashamed of this grossness once. "He who denies
flesh dies in the flesh." Anger's a city
where even his own lusts will not escape.
Anger's a citadel of hurt and revenge and rape.

Smile

Occasionally she saw a blemish.
Catherine would stop and open the door
as if light and air would work wonders
whereas likely as not they merely emphasized.
She did not let such things upset her. Like tight flowers
full of petals as crowded as her mouthful of teeth,
she arranged the necessary balance in things
so that even the clutter became composed.
Composure, though, was the real blemish.
Just when she thought the balance was achieved
something would happen—she would laugh too loud,
or too long, revealing those classically disorganised teeth.
A smile is not everything, but it is enough.
When she married, her poise was immaculate. The photos
threw a surprising focus on the husband
(usually a sober backdrop on these occasions):
his left front tooth was discoloured.
She flowered and was much loved
like one of those daisies crowded with petals.
None of us is without blemish, she would say,
and people thought of her as the exception.

Small gothic appetites

When she licked each finger he knew
what to expect. He didn't expect her to
plunge her bare hands into
the tomatoes and, dripping,
to advance upon him with a smile
he couldn't recognize.
"You like?" she said.
And he remembered the first time.
Then, though, it had been blood.

The grey lady of wonaminta

It is not that she is forgotten, the *Women's Weekly*
ran that article—wasn't it only ten years back? —
with the grey lady as its centrepiece, she doesn't lack
appreciation if that is what you mean. Already
though, I catch you out, stifling a smile, slightly
indulgent as if you suspected I might attack
you with a ghost or make a myth out of shadows. I lack
that sort of skill. I am not like the grey lady.

She came with my first wife. I thought of her as a bonus—
that colonial house in the Adelaide Hills. The dim
corridors and the sudden chill that announced she had come.
The grey lady is always serious. She will wait. As always the onus
is on us to believe or disbelieve. Of course you can smile
but come indoors, follow my footsteps this way for just a little
        while.

Colonial

She learned to accept the hot days. That
was the source. Heat dry as grey twisted logs
prepared in the sun for ancient rites, like
click click of stones before they split
suddenly: this is perspective,
the heat will be replaced with breezes and even rain
in patches. The time of flowering
will be miraculous, truly. The time of colour
will be slash of scarlet like a sabre across pallid flesh.
That is it, she thought.
It was a slow process that led her to this point
(not a Point but a dramatic Promontory)
and in the long afternoons in the front room
with the blinds drawn she had to become owner.
Without that premise all was lost.
Then, much later, she became the medium,
the agent of repetition as well as change.
She almost lingered on those hot days
to draw-in the very breathlessness of it
because she knew the pebbles might split.
But they were not everything. The change
was working its way
it might be irresolute but it was certain
and this smothering air was only the love feast
expressing within its urgency
only a flirtation with death.
Why that word?
In the crowded, darkened room
she was emerging as a judge
but her judgments were benign
(to her surprise) and even wilful.
When the rains did come, with autumn,
there were wonderful months
(why, in this hemisphere, did one refer
to months?) and, in the end,
it was the swarming hillsides
of native heath she would treasure and remember

even if the names she used were borrowed.
At least, she knew, she herself was borrowed.
That was when she turned herself into a ghost.
She was beginning to inhabit—finally—her property.

The painted shore

1.

Nothing important happened that day.
Alan swept the front path because the Chinese Elm leaves
fell like a giant's dandruff and he knew this was the time.
He relied on moisture and eventual earthworms to mulch.
He made himself another coffee. The telephone upstairs
beside his bed was silent. He had done everything.

He checked the double lock. He walked, as usual,
across the freshly swept path. Already more leaves.

2.

The Fleurieu Peninsula has its own sweetness
and its own melancholy. Sellicks Hill Range is a low wall
and its gentle contours fade under unblinking blue sky
asserting the perspective of infinity. That kind of landscape.
The coastal beaches are crumbling, erosion cliffs have
a reddish exhaustion. There is little expectation of green things.
These are beaches where individuals seem lost,
or if not lost, separated. Maslin's is the most beautiful
and the most lonely nude bathing beach in Australia.
Bodies separate from each other, even in crowded midsummer.
Spaces between individuals spread. The pitifulness of bodies
distinguishes this coastline. Further along, at Port Willunga,
the clothed bathers might as well be naked. They look vulnerable.

The Art Gallery of South Australia is holding an exhibition,
THE NAKED COAST, and Alan walks inside. These paintings
capture the edge of things. Beyond the edge: nothing given,
but attempts at domestication. Roads and cuttings.
Stalin in his Five Year Plans attempted to conquer the Steppes
with tractors and collective farms. Roads and cuttings.

It must be twelve years since Alan had stripped naked on Maslin's.
Mid-week. He was aware, first, of the feeling of lightness

upon his body, the way air felt places normally swathed in
     synthetics.
When his feet touched sand its softness between his toes caught
     him.
A few figures were scattered, sunning face down, or in single file.
Soon he was under the shadow of the cliffs. The sense of sun
     withdrawn
from his skin was as sensual as a shower. He stood, alone,
in shadow, coloured rocks above, his feet in shallow water.
He became aware that he was being watched. To think of your
     body
as the object of another's intent evokes curious sensations.
Alan was old enough to admit there was flattery. He held himself
straighter. He had pulled his tummy in. Now he smiled, for that.
Casually he strolled back into the sun. Suddenly,
in his early fifties, to be a tease. He had not glanced at the other
     man.
He paused to examine a rock pool. He stretched out his arms
as if to exercise. He splashed up the water. In all his life
Alan had never done these things. He flopped right into the water,
shallow and warm. It felt not only cleansing, but toned
all his muscles, massaging him. Later, back at the car
above the cliff-top, his clothes scratched his salty nipples
but as he started the motor the other man who was following him
arrived at the top of the cliff path, his arousal conspicuous.
In none of the paintings Alan has been looking at today
has the sense of isolation, loneliness and separateness of humans,
one from another, been absent from the landscape of that
     peninsula.
Twelve years. Alan carries it inside him as he lurches into the
     Mall.
He does not expect today to have a conversation with anyone.

3.

"Hello Alan, I'm looking for a decent record shop." Peter is
    English
and is a musician. He is always cheerful. "Am I holding you up?
I've just acquired this super new ultra-presto sound equipment
but all my CDs are back home of course." Alan offers to show Peter
a good shop. "It's the Mahler Third I crave. With Sinopoli.
That is my best favourite. You know, I lived in Switzerland
for a while. I was happy there. I was so happy. And the Mahler
    Third
brings back that feeling for me, always. That feeling of
    happiness."

"Happiness is always wonderful", says Alan. "And the Mahler is
    full
of alpine music." He thinks of happiness, and of the then and
    there
of how it catches you, sometimes by complete surprise.
"I hope you find your Mahler. I've just been to the Art Gallery
to look at an exhibition of paintings from the coast down here.
They are very gentle, imbued with the area. It's not a happy space,
it does not invite happiness. It invites, though, other things.
They have their own resonance."

"You must come over and listen to my new equipment. And the
    Mahler.
One evening. A glass of wine, and the wonderful Alpine music.
    Did I
tell you I was so happy that time, in Switzerland? This music
is still very special for me."

Only last night Alan had wept to hear the ending of *Der
    Rosenkavalier.*
He had remembered it conducted by the late Stuart Challender,
his last, before he died of AIDS. Those surprising tears last night.
How the body betrays us. How we are betrayed by the body.

Peter grabs Alan's hand and shakes it again. It is one of his
    gestures

every time they meet. "I'll give you a call. Come over."
They, both of them, must find many weekends isolated and
        isolating,
away from their own normal situations, here in Adelaide.

When Alan returns to his tiny flat the phone inside is ringing.
He fumbles with keys. The phone ceases
just as he pushes the door open.

II Four sestinas

Chekhov's Mongoose

Dr Chekhov was infatuated. This is the story.
Returning from the Russian prison isle of Sakhalin
where he circulated ten thousand questionaires and noted
with his usual dispassion the appalling conditions,
he made his first foray beyond Russian soil
via the China Sea. In Ceylon he acquired a mongoose.

It was lithe, tame and affectionate. It was quick, this mongoose,
and the doctor spent the homeward voyage like a story
out of a children's adventure, laughing, mopping its soil
and the broken crockery, replacing the memories of Sakhalin
with this new-found love. Without leash or chain, without
       conditions
to restrict its freedom, his pet became famous, more noted

(in that shipboard idyll) than Chekhov was, more noted
than any rival souvenirs: Siamese cat, monkey. His mongoose
loved him. When it broke all the rules and conditions
of social behaviour it turned dark soulful eyes, like a Story
Book Princess, and melted him with a look. Not even Sakhalin
with all its woes and tragedy could dredge from the dark soil

of its soul such pathos. Caught in his own soil
where ardour mixed with rancour, the good doctor noted
how vulnerable he was, and relented. Sakhalin
eased gently from his mind, replaced by a mongoose
which cried when it was left alone. The story
does not end there. Life has a way of imposing conditions.

When Chekhov returned, nothing was changed. The conditions
he fled from in Moscow—a demanding family, lovers, the grim soil
he had turned into rich prose in each celebrated story—
now returned to chill him. "When I come to visit", he noted,
"please be warned. I come with my pet mongoose
who is tamer than children, wilder than Sakhalin."

His published report, THE ISLAND OF SAKHALIN,
caused a sensation, and calls to reform penal conditions.
Life became a whirlwind again and though his mongoose
was the season's novelty, on his new Estate on the dark soil
of Malikhovo, it ran off. Yes, it was found, but he noted
the broken plates, the damage, the way every least story

mixes charm with wreckage. Some say it's Chekhov's own story.
Moscow's Zoo was, well, provincial. It was not noted
for health or for hygiene. Until 1893 it possessed no mongoose.

Sestina in the time of El Niño

It is the most beautiful day of the century
though all forecasts warn of drought and heat
but outside there is a breeze, a dappled light
and I have a cup of coffee in my hand, thinking
of other days that I once called beautiful
and how we can never get enough, though we are full.

Beautiful, though, is relative. The newspapers are full
of headlines which, at this end of the century,
are more cynical than filled with even the heat
of the moment—a landslide, a murder, a brief spotlight
on endangered mammals, a spontaneous and unthinking
media Princess whose death makes her beautiful.

We all know the story. What is not so beautiful
though is the packaging and presentation, full
of cellophane or gladwrap shine—apt for our century
of camera surfaces where only the heat
of arclamps ripens the gourmet fruit. "Shift the light
this way, Marcel. No, don't interrupt, I'm thinking!"

Just a few streets from my old home I keep thinking
of the fish-shop princess, now gladwrap beautiful
at a cost that must keep her consultant's coffers full.
She is the poor man's Diana, she is the End Of The Century
writ in red hair as honest as that arc-lamp's heat.
And she has a cause: bring bigotry into the light.

Television cameras whirr, she strides with clear delight
into the centre and, smiling at first, is already thinking
of how to dig up hate and make it beautiful,
of how to harness malice and make it full
of triumph, how to spend the lessons of this century
of manipulation so that flesh will blister in the heat

without losing the spotlight. It's alright. Heat
is what sells products, and if you smile at the light
right in your eyes no one will be thinking
of the consequences. Hate will seem beautiful,
petulance a charm (remember Diana?). Her smile stays full.
It is the most beautiful day of the century.

In this most beautiful day of the century
we stay indoors, glued to the gladwrap light,
held by the media princess whose poison cup is full.

Revival

Last night what I dreamed was the smell of you—
Incense smell, something precise: perhaps ripe fruit
Nearing softness in the windfall dark, perhaps
Even smell with a dry loft or a cellar in it,
Something of midsummer in a cold climate—it was sweet,
Touched with that further layer: dryness, darkness.

Out of something like twenty-five years of darkness,
Ready or not, your return was accurate, sweet
Excitement, so that in my sleep I played with it,
Mouthed it, licked and savoured. This was folly perhaps,
Either indulgent or indulged—but like the taste for fruit
My hunger was immediate. That hunger recognized you

Before memory had anything to do with it. You
Entered me then, your taste not your smell. Darkness
Remained irrelevant, we were back among windfall fruit
Touching and exploring young flesh—our own—so sweet,
Hot and responsive we were perhaps drunk, or perhaps
Each of us thought we were drunk. Once that was the word for it.

Feeling was the word for it, once. Oh yes, it
Overcame us, just as it overcame me now. You
Never came to my bed last night. Dreams are perhaps
Desperate short-circuits that disinter darkness
To make those long rotted apples immediate and sweet
Instead of mulch. This is not memory. These are real fruit.

Mere smell—immediacy of smell—it now involves fruit
Each of us once rolled among, laughing. Too much of it
Seeps back and knowledge is what makes that sweet
Wither and torture me. Why did I dream of you?
In all these decades that was over, done. Darkness
Tilled the fruit grove, chopped all those trees perhaps?

How, then, do I account for this? Even smell is perhaps
Modified over such a long time. It cannot be you, not the fruit
In that orchard, not the evening, later, full of darkness
Clothing our intimacy with feel, not sight. Yet it
Knows immediately every detail. How could you
Still be a breath I swallowed eagerly, young and sweet?

Tonight I will dream an old sweetness, even though you
Ought to reel at my sagging flesh. At night, perhaps,
Wizened fruit may still smell alive in all the darkness.

Australian Horizons

The strangled high voices of Australian men
again and again remind me of barbed wire
and the wind twanging for distance. Then
I remember the eyes of Australians squinting
as they might be, say, behind windscreens or in traffic
with sun glare and sun mirage in their eyes.

Distance is hard to get out of Australian eyes.
Even in cities there's a bit of dust on the tongue, and men
keep a bit of silence under the armpit. Sometimes in traffic
there's the old childhood, twanging like wire:
and even city kids know the sense of paddocks squinting:
Australia's a burr that itches right into you, then.

High voices are for distance. You yell out, and then
you listen and wait. There is dust in your eyes
as well as on your tongue. The threat of silence squinting
still pinches to treble the voices of Australian men.
Memory is tight as the vibrations of fencing wire
even in Sydney with its high whine of endless traffic.

4 p.m. in the Public Bar, and it's busy traffic
alright. The itch mounts. It is getting higher. Then
memory clicks. This is beyond Sydney, the sound hits wire
back in the haze of distance and you squint your eyes
as if you had just walked in. Like iron filings, men
are drawn to the magnet of habit. They're squinting.

Once in Venice near the Grand Canal I caught the squinting
high male voices of Australians, dusty in the traffic
of foreign pedestrians. They herded together, six men
and their wives. I felt the sweat of their armpits and then
the way they bunched tighter. There were gates in their eyes
and their defensive silence was taut as barbed wire.

Their women dived for shops, picked up glass and wire
souvenirs, went further afield. They peered then returned
        squinting
to the Tourist Menu outside the Trattoria. The blokes kept their
        eyes
narrow as a field of seeds or the dotted lines in traffic.
They clung and were defensive. Their distance then
was absolute and inflexible. There were burrs in those men

and their voices were tight. They'd not left home at all but were
        men
rolling pellets of dust under the tongue to become wire
high pitched in empty paddocks, blinking and squinting.

III   The visions

Letters from Gwen Harwood

Letters prove to us we once cared

JANET MALCOLM : *The Silent Woman*

Be suspicious of letters, all you researchers.
When she wrote to me, when I wrote back to her,
there were mirrors in the text as well as candour,
there was the delight in sharing as well as the riches
we uncover from ourselves just in the scratches
of words done by hand. They uncover
associations as much as repercussions
and a play that twists the noses of theoreticians.

What took my breath, what scratched my eyes with grief,
though, a week after her death, were her perky cards
and her letters with the snail-trail feel of words
exposed to an indifferent air. Messages from life
as it was happening, they lead to an empty shell
where the patterns sparkle but there is no muscle at all.

The Dream of return

i.m. Gwen Harwood

Back, back to stand in the school playground
in the January heat with those last scarlet flowers
of the coral tree littering the sandstone ridge
and those black poinsiana seedpods the smell
and colour of hot bitumen—there are places she haunts,
a tangible ghost, and they are all Brisbane.

Her dream is to stand in the midst of everything
with a silver comb in her hand and a bauhinia
resting like a butterfly on her shoulder.
She will be warm again, drenched in living sweat
that cools and leaves her skin bathed in shadows;
she will have returned to the childhood rip of rainwater
after storms and the afternoon sea breeze
—her oldest lover—blessed as heaven itself,
as if it had been eating red carnations by the dozen
and yellow allamanda all morning
and its breath will have the Pacific Ocean
to remind her of every summer holiday.

That living breeze will, as always, be a physical God
who has scattered spray and run naked out of the surf
then gazed at the long glittering beach, laughed,
opened his mouth and swallowed everything
before spreading the wings that will carry him
as the one God right to her doorstep
and into her arms, which would open wide with the
innocence of childhood and its quick sensuality.

That dream of a breeze which cools even hot asphalt
is her original godhead and its memory is stronger
than this Hobart morning, with its skittering rain
and another vicious nip from the antarctic.

This is the sustaining dream, it is the taste
and the flavour that would carry her back,
back to that flowering tree where she would be safe
in her first Paradise, back to where she would drink
at the first sparkling waterfall, eat her first lunch
under the Coral Tree, back to where she would
have her long thirst finally quenched and back,
where the breeze from the sea would keep its promises,
back, back to where she would never be hungry again.

After twenty years

It's hard work, maintaining a rainbow.

Flies, for instance, who would have costed-in
those little irritating familiars?
Though everyone knows (after the event)
that they invade anything
and a rainbow isn't exempt—
it's a free slide.

Then there is the business of reflections.
The double-rainbow glimpsed then and now
and remembered back from the best positions—
on Mount Agung, or that time down the canyon
on 42nd Street with the air so suddenly clean
and rinsed as if we were not only forgiven
but blessed.
Reflections, though, have poison tips
to their arrows.

The domestic rainbow is wonderful enough
perhaps even for the twentieth time
but comes that moment when the knives tear in
screaming "Rainbow! Rainbow outside!"
and you don't shrug
but you don't move either.
That very evening snails consume your lettuce
and your favourite CD goes silent,
the wonderful Bogart video skitters out of control
and it is your own hair clogging the downpipe.

Rainbows outlive you, and that's a problem,
for all their suddenness and their unfamiliarity.
It is true, certain waterfalls project rainbows
like a light switch, but nobody yet
has patented the supermarket model
or even the boutique variety.
Like marriage, rainbows prepare for a long haul

and many silences. Like silence
they remind you of hard work. And perhaps
you do go outside, after all, brushing away flies.

Stag in the upstairs parlour

The decoration's genteel—beige
and Regency, imitation dried flowers
with a ribbon. The deer was once real.

Shoulders to eight-pointed antlers,
he intrudes out of the wall
and out of all proportion.
It's not that the room is caged;
it might have been unremarkable.

We are meant to believe in trophies.
That ancient fear of humans means
those false eyes are upturned.
Some taxidermist
would have been paid well.

Was there smell? —
stag in rut, saliva, hoof
stench and heavy breath?
In this upstairs parlour
all is a model of preservation.
The cedar, polished to perfection,
had been tree for a thousand years.

We think of a forest
but it could have been some local scrub
("The deer, gift of Her Majesty
in Balmoral"). We imagine
the sudden rifle, a crack
harsh as a loud cough, as immediate.

Energy and lust.
Bone antlers with points
tug the covers back. Polish
does not preserve, it is
a brackish pool. Dried flowers.

Poem for John Olsen

1.

The way we learned the sun
was to look at shadows.
When shadows move
they carry the smells of the earth with them
they wear the sun on their backs.
When shadows crawl back
over stones so hot they click their teeth
that is when we know the sun
stands over us and pisses its light.
We call the light many names
but they all mean that even the stones
have a language
and the sun's waste is our energy.
Shadows are among us already
fingering the earth because they know
all things the sun casts away
are recyclable.

2.

We threw those river-sticks
onto the coals. Stones
underneath crouched, impatient
for the end of the picnic
but storing the heat obediently.
They let the potatoes be poked in
and the yams and the black kettle.
We sang raucous songs
and then ones with the night in them
so that the embers would glow
and we would remember. Later
stars became as inquisitive
as mist from the riverbed across the sandbank.
But by then we had eaten
and we took into us just what we needed

which was quickness and stillness
and the proximity of each other
just this once. Words are stars:
when you close your fingers around them
they become impossibly remote.

But the river-sticks offered us ash
in the end, and we were fat with our meal
and the silence was fat and comfortable
and the stones still carried the warmth
for a long time yet.

When darkness is the stage
shadows say nothing, it is the light
that flickers and we say words like
'radiant'. Absence
was always a sensuous teacher.

3.

Day with all the time in the world
hours of it
draws wet shadows out of the ashes
and begins with treetrunks
and then grasstrees
and even the split stones in the fireplace,
it sends their shadows out to reclaim dryness
to make sure every surface will be actual
so that nothing the night did will be remembered
although the earth is incapable of true silence.
Sunshine, though, has a way
to make you blink
to blind you, even,
and morning is just beginning.

It's at night we talk about language
because we believe in silence as a means of hoarding things.

Daytime, without question we think energy,
attack, what to do next.
We are waiting for orders.
We are a sport in the shadow, ants underfoot.
The sun wakes with a full bladder.
It plays games with us. We
are grateful for anything.

Thirteen ways of remembering the river

1.

Look! I acknowledge
that you taught me escape,
and ways of release.
You were there from the start
and I was your child
from the first moment.
That was a baptism.
It was not escape,
it was recognition.

2.

I am an inland son,
not a beach person
or a person of ice and mountains.
But, inland, the river
is powerful, even
a river that moves in shade
and shallows, that drought
threatens or that floods
overwhelmingly
in its own seasons.

3.

You were there in me
so far back I cannot remember
a time I did not know the creek
and its slippery rocks
and the life in the water.
I think I was always aware
there was death in the water.

4.

Caution and adventure
—the allure of water
is its untrustworthy
balance. We float
and we drown or discover
that we swim
that the effect of floating
is to enhance the life
we discover in our own body.

5.

My father taught me to float
steadying me gently with his hand.
That was at Lynches' Crossing
where the river sand
slipped into the water
and there were doublebars and zebra finches
among the riverbank thickets.
I took my first swimming strokes
by myself, I discovered power.

6.

Or the time when Berne Tooth panicked
out too deep and we both struggled
as if the water was eager
to get us entangled. There were slippery weeds
down there. The taste of water
was suddenly more bitter than salt
though we were weeks away from the sea.
Someone caught us up. The river
knew it must wait.

7.

It was only weeks later
on School Parade that we were warned
of the danger of swimming.
One of the Grade 5 boys
had been drowned, wagging it
over at Lynches' Crossing.

8.

In my teen years the river
was our Saturday adventure.
On bikes we ventured further
to Colleges' Crossing or to Kholo
small groups together
swinging from ropes out to the middle
teasing the girls, laughing,
awkward as the dog we threw in,
playful as the surface ripples
when the afternoon breeze
made its regular appearance
sending down bottlebrush flowers
that floated lazily downstream.

9.

We floated lazily downstream
on long river branches rescued from driftwood
high on tangled trunks,
evidence of last years' floods.
Paddling easly we passed cliffs
and water meadows, the gravel pit
and the ghost cave someone said
still held traces of Aboriginal artefacts.
The water showed us miles of riverbank
with no sign, mostly, of habitation.
It was the river itself became the centre.
Whole weekends were built around it.
When we trudged, or swam, back upstream
we were still wet with sweat
so that the last plunge in
up at the swinging pool
made us feel we owned the river
or the river owned us.

10.

In the adult years
we didn't need the obvious river.
But it was always just beyond the paddocks
or over the rise, flowing casually
and with its own momentum.
Once you are aware of the river
as a live movement you know the pulse
and it outpaces your own breath
although, like breath, it promises certainty.

11.

Certainty is an illusion. The big flood
that finally rose was wider and wilder
than the mystical 'flood of 1893'
I grew up with Grandma's memories of.
River as power. River as revenge.
River as death.
That schoolkid entangled in snags
back at Lynches' Crossing
was just another ghost.
The river has its images.

12.

When I look back
I see forward. I acknowledge
the river and its baptismal font.
Baptism's a beginning
but all rivers move to an end.
Passage is their definition
although repetition is what carves out their beds.
Embedded in that thought
the river's blessing locates itself
as portent as well as parable.
No wonder I do not escape
from the memory of river water
or the stink of it on my flesh.

13.

When I was young and lusty
there were certain days midweek
when I would escape from work
and drive to Allawah, the reach
above College's Crossing.
There I would swim naked.
I was joined to the river
and to the place and within the land.
Who is to say that was not
a way of reconciling life and death?
I will never come to that place again
but that is not to say
it is lost or that the river
did not receive my seed.

IV Travel

Belgrade, 1989

"This city has been razed 27 times." My host
walks with me through the park that overlooks
the junction of the Danube and the Sava. "Our books
are all records of oppression and survival. We lost
so many times our treasures and our freedom, and the cost
has always been crushing. But loss is what makes
us resilient. We will survive. The victor takes
our spoils but not our heartland. That we value most."

Children with guns attack us. He laughs. "These are only toys."
But for them the toys are real, and their faces mean business.
There is no concession. Old women with kerchiefs raise useless
hands to protect their wares—aprons and embroideries—
but the kids are gone already, as if this park were craters
again, and they were the new generation of enemy eaters.

Pristina, Kosovo

"Kosovo is a hallowed place for Serbs."
My guide thumps the steering-wheel. We are driving
through a green landscape but the hills
are clambering back towards the mountains.
"In 1683 our King was forcing back the Turks.
But he was killed." Four hundred years of occupation
glint in his face. "It was the turning point.
But we remember it still. In Kosovo province
we have the oldest and most venerated monastries."

That is where we are heading for. I have seen
reproductions of those strong muscled angels
with their many-coloured wings, eagle-like
and illustrating strong upthrust and capable flight,
not pallid levitation at head-height into a whitewashed room.
"We still do not forgive those Serbians who weakened
and converted to the faith of the enemy."

As we approach Pristina, the capital, he points out
the walled farmhouses. They are seemingly everywhere.
"Those are the Albanians They fled their land
and have settled here. In two generations they have multiplied
—they breed families like farm animals, 20, 24, more.
Now they have become similar to rabbits or feral cats
in your country—I have cousins in Melbourne."
He takes me direct to the new University of Kosovo.
It has just opened. I admire a scalloped architecture
surmounted by dozens of domes, more than dozens;
they echo the Byzantine churches, but also, I note,
the neighbourhood Mosques. It is all glass
and filigree. I am invited in.

That was in 1985.
　　　　　　Near century's end I have learned
that Albanians in Kosovo are now banned from that University.
When I was there it was the first time my poems
were read aloud in English, Serbian, Albanian.
I bought a cassette of folk music from the province.
It sounded Arabic, but the old singer
was Albanian.

Fishing Lake Ochrid

Of course there is ecological concern. This
is an aware environment, we love the lake and its fish,
we point out to strangers their uniqueness. Rush
to the restaurant, we say, and taste: you will surely rejoice
in the pink flesh of a living fossil, you will kiss
with your lips that specialty. We wish
for our visitors at least that much content. The dish
on your plate is history. It's sold at a modest price.

Two days a month it is legal to fish but of course
often the guardians of fish poaching are the most guilty.
Today my son-in-law came home with a bounty
of three large trout. As a distinguished guest there has
to be a banquet in your honour. You have praised
our fish: to supply the table all means have been used.

Dried watermelon

In Uzbekistan where more than half
the land is desert and half the rest is thrown
into the great chain of Tienchan
melons are special, globes of compressed life.
Markets are full of merchandise, gruff
dramatic traders in the stalls will offer one
of the pomegranates, persimmons, pears, or lean
slivers of watermelon pared with a swift knife.

I bought in the free markets of Tashkent
ridgy chunks, compressed and apple-brown,
dried melon intense as sunlight, thick as stone
and hoarding its taste, its surprising nourishment.
More than taste: between seed and pith and skin
Uzbekistan itself seemed the flavour clambering in.

Samarkand by moonlight

We drive from the airport after dark.
"This road", our guide says, "was the road
of the old silk routes. We celebrated
two thousand five hundred years, the area
was ceded to Russia in 1867. In 1917
the Revolution began in Registan square."

Registan, where Moslems held ceremonial executions
and the astronomer Ulugbec built the first Madrash,
his school for boys.

Marco Polo praising its beauty. Tamurlaine
buried in the Gur Emin Mausoleum: in the early light
we clatter over cobblestones.

We are an official party. "In Registan the Moslem women
burned their veils, it was 1924. We now are a centre
for education. Before 1917 that was only for boys."

Semi-sweet, half acrfid smell of heat and vegetation.
At Gur Emin Mausoleum there are three boys
under a mulberry tree. When we reach our hotel
we look over the great blue-starred dome
hunched in moonlight like shadows of stars
in the gourd of night.
Black shapes rise suddenly like giant bats,
in hundreds, then hundreds, then hundreds.

They resettle in the trees below us: ravens,
fruit and foliage entirely replaced by ravens
shouldering each other. Vast colonies
have become rustling leaves. Samarkand by moonlight
settles them again in the uncommon streets
to wait for some lone pedestrian,
the next victor.

At Methoni

Down in the west beyond Arcadia and Olympia
Methoni is as far as our hire car goes.
Almost nothing here. Stunted cork trees,
girls on the back of goat carts selling cherries
knotted into glowing forearms with tight dimples
like some ancient declaration of the seed goddess.
Boys looking for shade. Methoni
is where the Adriatic pulls things down
to shoreline, cliff, fort.
                              The walls
of some Venetian enterprise after these years
have the look of permanence though the locals joke.
         A narrow causeway, a lookout tower, we explore
Frankish tunnels, wells, keep, tower
and see Turkish bath house additions,
pits, something from the German Occupation.
I take your photograph among red poppies,
golden everlastings. The mount might be propitious
or the lode from earlier excavations.
Our age likes to dig and pretend the difference.
Almost nobody here. The many centuries gather
into a sparse, thick knot, like cherries round the core
of the farmgirls' handiwork. We deflect
to the Taverna; our host
catchs the accent between us, waves us to our place.
Yes, he lived in Melbourne until he saved for this.
And yes, this is his home though the sons are still
over there. We nod to the Mediaeval fortress
and ask questions. No, there is someone in the village
perhaps tomorrow. Tonight, see, this special fish.
It is large, fresh caught, just for us,
at a special price.

Venice

Snow scuffing the black gondolas.
The way silence makes our footsteps clatter
over cobbles. "No cars", you remark
and we congratulate ourselves as if
this is the way it should be. Winter
and the coldness of water tugging our shoes.
The palaces are shuttered. Palladio
slips inside leaving only facades
and the lap of water over worn stairs.
You shiver. I take your gloved hand
in my own. Soon we will be back
to the little room in the Albergo
with the canal water breathing on
our window. Are we lost?
Walking in Venice is always a hazard.

Hazardously, we cross another bridge
and hope we are right. When the Grand Canal
reaches the end of the street we grin.
Told you so. Dark so early—inside
that gloomy building across the water
there are lights, chandeliers, a fresco
by Tintoretto, wooden trunks closed up
with treasures no one has opened for a hundred years
—the lost score of *Ariadne* by Monteverdi, perhaps,
or letters from Liszt, Wagnerian velvet.
Outside, we might as well conjure the lot.

The snow is getting thicker though it melts.
Just before we turn inside to the tourist bill
and the rising damp, another black gondola
moves silently. A giant bronze horse
—one of the restored Cavalli of St Marks—
is strapped in. Snow tickles its haunches.
It might be heading for Constantinople
but it is enough to have seen it

in this real snow, unobserved
by all the richly shuttered windows.

For Alexamnder Pushkin

You African, Pushkin, you Russian,
and of course you who come with salt
and bread to confound me: how can I refuse
you? Not even Princesses could say 'Halt!"

But I tell you this. I have seen your room,
I have caught not the chill but the delight
of your past. They say the temperature drops
in the presence of ghosts. I flushed there, alright.

I burned in the eagerness, like cards flung-down
(the Queen of Spades, perhaps?); in that presence
though it was an ordinary day with tourists and tickets
you moved quickly. You were of the essence.

Fantasy? Perhaps. But in a corner alone
was the old auntie, the sort always clicking her lips
at cloakrooms or sweeping up cigarettes.
She shuffled and I saw her. There are times the heart stops.

No, of course she could not have been Pushkin's nurse,
telling him fables and fantasies. But the door leapt open
and Baba Yaga grinned. Oh, that's only the beginning, she said,
and I knew almost anything was about to happen.

V At Fassifern

Four Sestinas

The ghost rock pool

When I was a kid, if the swelter of summer provided
prickly-heat and a warfare with clothes, someone
would say "Give it all back to the blacks, it's blackfella country"
and we'd dream of air-conditioning, and iced water
and beer, and out-of-town the heat would settle
and shade would flatten, and we'd still keep plodding on.

We were nine-to-five servants with wristwatches strapped on.
We were sweating onto the cash-books, our print marks provided
next year's auditors with smalltown diversions: someone
would say "Well over the century that day, the country
fried for a week", and we'd remember hot water
out of the cold-water tap, and the auditors would smile, then
        settle.

We were still wearing ties round our necks, though we'd settle
for something easier out of sight of customers. On
hot days, later, there was a fashion for shorts, provided
we wore long socks. Safari Suits appeared. Someone
set the trend and things take a long time in country
places—to arrive or to die. We still drank warm water.

"Give it all back to the blacks"—but tepid water
still quenches thirst and we slogged it out. We'd settle
for thoughts of a dip in the creek or the baths, on
those summer days. It was a hot drive but it provided
us with dreams of long moments of coolness, and someone
always spoke of a rockpool hidden upcountry.

We lived in the imagination of that place, that country
rockpool surrounded by shade trees, with ice-deep water
below the surface where bottlebrush pollen would settle
and insects would hover. It was something to fantasize on
as the afternoon sweltered and until the first breeze provided
thoughts of escape. A rockpool diver has to be someone.

A rockpool diver is no clerk, he is free, he is someone
at one with the land, he has assumed the country
by the work of imagination and the magical gift of water.
On those hot days, despite ourselves, we began to settle
for blackfella country, and the same dreams that lured us on
and inhabited us were dreams that acknowledgment provided

and we never gave a thought to the image of someone
quick as a watersnake or with heels hard as that rock country
and with gleaming dark skin diving and laughing in that water.

Cycle

When we were kids everything was home
for as far as our legs took us. The unending
backyard with the six mango trees and the weather
discoloured fence was limitless. Forget
the mozzies and the sandflies, on those almost brutal
afternoons we played there until the onset of night.

When we progressed to scooters and then bikes, night
was what brought us, reluctantly, back to the lights of home,
and the hot kitchen, the family meal and the brutal
Radio News—battles and Wartime with their unending
promise of Victory and their gloomy stories. We'd forget
the world outside the wireless. We'd forget the weather,

crouched down to listen. Our parents were quiet. The weather
of life-and-death was taught 7 o'clock at night
and every night. I still cannot forget
the switch to attention at that News fanfare. Home
was the refuge alright, but we learned the unending
threat of News voices. News was always to be brutal.

Adolescents, in the '50s, our motorbikes made brutal
assertions in the suburb. Out in all weather
(rain stung like needles) we discovered the unending
power of movement. We burned up the night
in that decade post-war, when to stay home
was a sneer. The momentum was up, don't forget.

Later, even cars and their comforts failed to forget
the two-stroke, the four-stroke decade. We learned to be brutal
then, but we also were moving so far out of home
that we vanished and were as predictable as weather
and we did return, sticky with hunger and the night
winked and was tolerant and it all seemed unending

though timing was all. The cycle is not really unending,
merely sufficient to prove that we need not forget
all the paces, the classes, the voices. Night
confines as much as it opens. Peace can be brutal
and war can be as unremarkable as weather.
Weather, though, was what first brought us home

and it is strange, and perhaps brutal, to think of home
as having this unending lien on the weather,
especially as we forget so many things in a good night.

Growing pains

If it was old, we didn't want to know. NOW
was all that mattered and it stretched out before
us like the holidays or like the Pacific Ocean.
We plunged into the surf and nobody would believe
the taste of salt on lips, or that shoulders sprayed with sun
would ever be less than the sum of the moment, or even more.

We lived for this. Even last year was no more
than dried shells in a shoebox under the bed. NOW
thumped outside and over the sand it was the sun
racing the breeze to the sandhills, calling us before
breakfast and urging us out. Last year? We couldn't believe
how young we were then. This year we were Lords of the Ocean.

This year had one new promise. Tomorrow. Like an ocean
feeling its tides and its rips, we began to sense more
than the sandhills and immediate surf. We began to believe
in some muscular future, we were beginning, now,
to look at ourselves and at others. We had been children before,
running and twisting, happy to be just free in the sun

and reckless as fish in the water. If we stayed in the sun
too long it was our skin told us, not parents. The ocean
schemed with us, it was immediate as seaweed. When it darkened
        before
a storm, the piled seawrack tomorrow would be more
than enough. But something had changed. When we walked out
        now
after a storm, it was our own turbulence we had to believe.

When Tomorrow seeps into your blood you taste salt. To believe
in the future you have to find old things under the sun
and you feel the tides surging up through your own body now
and that's a direction: it is out. It is away. You are an ocean
and you're only beginning to sense the currents, they tug you
        more
and more violently, seriously, than you ever dreamed before.

NOW is reduced. Tomorrow is stretching and throbbing before
you, unexpected in its dread and its allure. If you believe
in it (as you must) you are drowned in its ocean. More:
you begin to acknowledge the restless past of the sun,
you are bound in the ancient tides and the limiting ocean
and to a past that begins its task of erosion now.

The sun glitters on ocean. It was old before
your first swim, your first holiday. There are no more
holidays. What you believe in your blood will define you now.

The Fassifern

That name itself suggests a sandy creek,
shade of bottlebrush or blackbean or feathery
wattle—in summer there will be certainly snakes
and if you're lucky you'll catch the flick and ripple
of a platypus in the larger pools. Tiny fish
or yabbies will tickle bare toes. This is boyhood.

Boyhood is always hot, it is summer. Boyhood
knows where to find all the big pools in the creek,
it is excited by the old stories of the gigantic fish
a river cod not seen since Oxley—but that feathery
shadow has not gone away. Boyhood knows every ripple
might lead to the catch. Boyhood also teases snakes.

But in the mottled creeks of the Fassifern, snakes
bask in their own priority. This extends further than boyhood
and is a part of the country that makes town boys a mere ripple
over the surface. The Fassifern keeps secrets in each creek
and though the shallows may be dappled and feathery
now, past holds its own shadows, like the giant brooding fish.

When we scrambled down the bank in a rush to fish
or to swim or simply to escape like wrigglers or snakes
into the delight of water, our noise was like parrots, feathery
bright but raucuous and squabbling. We asserted boyhood
with laughter and punches and thought nothing of it. It was our
        creek
and when we got there it obeyed us. We were shadows, a ripple.

We never coaxed out the mythical cod, though we did catch the
        ripple
of platypus and sometimes the flash of a kingfisher. We were the
        fish
excited by movement and sunlight. But we did learn that creek
or its aspects, and we even developed a caution with snakes
—it took only one scare. We were trapped in our boyhood
like the kingfisher and parrot in their own brilliant feathers.

The creek was the smallest part of the Fassifern, tail feathers
or wingtip—the valley spread richly all round. Its creek,
even so, gathered everything in and defined it. Even in boyhood
somehow we understood that. We accepted the mythical fish
as a sacred emblem without question. We allowed the snakes
their ancient right of passage before us to the creek.

The Fassifern returns to this, gathering snakes, a creek,
feathers on the sand, platypus or fish—a ripple
somewhere. Boisterous bare bodies. Summer. Boyhood.

VI   For Dorothy my mother

Figs

Patty Brown had freckles, she had small eyes
and mottled teeth. She stole things.
She was two years older but
her backyard was next-door
and there weren't any other kids for streets.
We had six mango trees. They had a fig.

Our mangoes were the old sort, turpentine
and stringy, and they left a sting
in the corners of your mouth.
Her fruit were wrinkled and brown
but we knew they were special, she would fold
hers open to reveal the tender flesh inside.
Six ripe mangoes were her trade for one fig.

Had our mangoes been Bullock Heart
the new Bowen variety, that would be different;
one Bullock Heart would be worth
anything Patty Brown could think of.

Patty always won. When
I did trade for one of her figs
I usually threw it to the chooks.
The taste was almost nothing.
Even when we received the fruit
we didn't know how to approach the matter.
For some fruit, you need experience.

Then

With a silver comb in her hair and a handful of promises
she was the grandmother of all grandmothers
and the headmistress of all my childhood hopes and wishes.
She was large in the kitchen and her steak and kidney pie
made mum's efforts something we learned to scorn.
Her sponge cakes were fairyfloss, her ice cream
(whipped up in a wooden tub) made ours seem flat and flaky.
She controlled everything. My grandfather sat
in the tobacco stained Chesterfield and listened to Parliament.
Or he hobbled outdoors to throw corn at the chooks.
He had a nicotine moustache and a few jokes
that he always ribbed us with. We loved him.
My grandmother kept us busy. She always had expectations
and when she and my spinster aunt took us on long tramrides
they would end up quarrelling, their voices rising, tempers
      flaring
louder than black drums or a highway crash.

Old Tom song

When I was young
I stamped the floor
and said "Excuse me
please, but I am sure
I've heard that tired old song before."

And when I grew
and so did you
I said, "Come off it
Blue, I thought you knew
we've got to change it, make it new."

But long before
they shut the door
I thought, "Wait on
a bit, I'm damned well sure
that song ends something like *encore encore*."

So now when those
we know get up my nose
I say, "*Encore!*"
and so it goes,
the leaf, the rose,
and Old Tom Cobley I suppose.

Three sonnets on death

1.

Death does not understand the out and in of breath,
it listens to the newborn cry and hears the first
instalment of the lease, it weighs up terms and interest
with its computer logic. It juggles with
the simple binaries—so different from earth
recycling everything to save the best till last
and generous to a fault with sex and famine and feast;
earth takes death and reshapes it back to birth.

Death is the simple thump of an average drum
without syncopation. Death is the single note
that will deafen your ear. It is the common chord, the weight
that flattens everything. Death is the debt-collector come
to the front door who knows only the instructions to hand.
Death does not look inside. Death does not understand.

2.

The computer does not lie. But neither does it tell the truth.
The computer has learned speed, and precision, and to obey.
It exists outside time but it can be scheduled the way
clocks can be scheduled. It can be confused in ourselves with
speed and circumlocution which is why it is both
enviable and appalling. No wonder we tend to say
the compurer is Little Bastard or the Big Okay.
It's we who invented irony. Machines mimic death.

But death in the shape of absence: the non-breath,
the black-or-white alternatives, the use of energy
without that human nuance, that throb in the voice, that synergy
between a dozen fingers imperfectly combining with
a dozen violin-strings to make the sound musical, not
mechanical.
It's we who respond. Machinery, finally, is impractical.

3.

We do not understand death. We worship machines
but that's not to say we really worship them.
We welcome them, we invite them into our home,
we exploit them ruthlessly. With death, we are the ones
who feel the lower hand—we laugh, but that defines
our unease. That odd machine, death, has come
a long way to call us each by name:
this is the right address? The contract ends.

Once there were temples and monuments to death.
But I imagine a computer bank with all
the air-conditioning disfunctional,
the energy sources immobilized, and the path
already flickering from the screen, and no breath
of air, no trace of smell, no memory of earth.

Tree

That first summer the hot air was so delicate we melted
our skins became underwater volcanoes our eyes blinked salt
and the soap of our fingerprints slid till our embrace felt
like danger. Outside, from the relentless west nothing faltered
but I considered the options. Our view was the west. I planted
that avenue of Portugese Elms, Celtis Sinensis. They did not wilt
then, they were arms and then torsos. They were the pelt
of the green god in our clumsy clay. They shot up. They sheltered.

On the sixth summer we held a party under the big trees.
The heat had grown indelicate but we were screened by branches
that flexed above to sun themselves and squat on their haunches.
We laughed our laughter and we clinked our sparkling ice.
Years later I drove past that place. The valley had grown foreign
with seedling trees, infesting the western slope. They were our
    own.

Tenant

He had the phone installed
but no one called.
He walked out for the mail
without fail
and walked back empty-handed
stranded.

It's not a matter of social stress;
that's anyone's guess.
It's not a matter of social chatter
—all that patter—
and it's certainly not a matter of pride
that he feels denied.

The great friendships inside his head,
can they be dead?
He looks at his fingers. He spreads them wide.
Touch is denied.
The past was always made to last.
It holds him fast.

There's always a gain when something has died:
be honest. Don't hide.
He walks back in. Each ghost
becomes a host.
He never makes an outside call.
Can that be all?

Skin as the parchment

It has happened,
the map and parchment of my skin
across the bones of my hand
(that is what we see first)
now folds into crocodile creases
or the scaly roughness of old maps.
I cannot see the back of my neck
which is the site, I am told,
of the defining pattern of old men—
Well, my hair has thinned
with as theatrical a gesture
as make-up artists might relish
and my beard is almost
truly white—theatre
in itself—so why wince
at the corrugations of skin
and its emphasis on surfaces?
      I remember a sudden glimpse
      when I was 37 and in New York
      of a woman not so much older
      in a poetry group. Animated,
      she leant toward me
      and I saw the curve
      that predicted her breasts:
      parchment, crocodile, wrinkled.
      Age curdles that memory
      and its sexual embellishment,
      energy caged
      in a network of wire, the mesh
      irrevokable and tightening
      the surface loosening.

Skin of the hand

Why ask the hand to do more? to be
more than it is, to hold more than enough
every time you reach out to touch or to be tough
or to crush and cuddle? The hand should be free
to express itself as texture simply. We see
no further than this—what the independent life
of each finger amounts to is flashing the knife
of clumsy messengers, complaining passively

or—let's face it—cycling around in the old
ruts without enterprise. When did you last
trust in touch? When were you unambiguously lost
in the wonder of tactile reality? Hot? or cold?
The five messengers come back home and let
their prints and parables express themselves as sweat.

Writer in public

I open my mouth, and seventeen yards of adhesive
myth falls out. Shut up, quick. But it's there,
sprawling out into everything, touching far
too many clean decisions to make. Am I really passive?

I open my feelings. Quick! The feeling's addictive
that I'm trapped. Seventeen yards of mirror, it's more
than even the best book could have bargained for.
I open my mouth. This time the silence is massive.

After the voice clears up the matter of accent,
volition, plans for the cards not on the table,
it trips up alright on the sticky past. Our words dabble
in magics, and a list for the butcher graphs out lines of descent
from a highway of dictionaries. I open my misgivings:
the highway tilts. There are voices, titterings, welcomings.

Making the news

I woke up this morning
and there was no news
no news at all
the papers were tossed
into the garden as usual
missing the rosebush
I heard the newsboy's bike
as he veered over the kerb
this was also normal
and had I turned on the radio
there would have been fanfares
and news flashes
but, even so, this morning
only the news itself was absent
it would have none of us.

What happened, instead,
was that people starved
in places that are on maps
that there was racial conflict
with breakages and old indignations
as well as indignities

there was an earthquake somewhere
flooding in unexpected places
and drought elsewhere
children were forced into pitiful labour
plain girls were raped as if
looks were not the question
and there was the usual catalogue
of business defections, fraud,
and outright exploitation
(as if it might ever be otherwise)
fortunes were lost
on the stock exchange
greed was pampered to
as if consequences
are always abstract

as if numbers and figures
            have powerful meaning
                        or have none
as if what we do
            in the morning
                        will leave us
and somehow become itself
            independent
                        like children

even though our own children
            take some pride in owning us
                        or embarrassment
which is the same thing
            expressed with more
                        animation
and what we do is not news
            that much we know
                        enough to be certain
while all the time
            uncertainty
                        is what is the real news
which is why
            I open the paper
                        in the kitchen
the same way
            as I pour a coffee
                        or think of toast—
secure in the habit
            of scanning headlines
                        skimming pages
and ignoring the advertisements
            which are always certain
                        and never certain enough.

It is as if
        nothing has happened
                today or last night
and it is out of this
        perhaps more than anything
                that news is born
or is about to be born
        or is beginning
                its long journey
so that tomorrow
        or the day after
                or even later
I will open the paper
        and be shocked.
                The end will be horrible.
I will lap it up
        I will lick my buttery fingers
                scanning the lines
and I will be happy at last
        the world re-connects
                I will feed on disorder.

For Dorothy my mother

1.

My mother died at ninety. In her last year
her eyes were so blurred there was no place
for smiles.

2.

My first memory is my mother's tea-leaves,
double used with half a spoonful
of crisp dry makings to 'freshen them up'.
I was born in the Depression.
We had toys made from cottonreels and string.
Shirts and pants were from cast-offs.
Flour came in 2lb. bags
handkerchiefs were made from those.
We were not poor
but waste was immoral and nobody knew
where tomorrow would lead, she said.

It led to the War,
full employment and an air-raid shelter
where our own sandpit had been.
Photographs show we had trikes then
but I remember the shelter in its dug-out
and the emergency rations, the first-aid kit,
and the mould on them. It was never used in panic.
When the siren did sound that once, my mother said
she preferred bombs to the cobwebs.

3.

Cakes and biscuits: these were the years of sugar
even when it was rationed. My mother
stands in her flat-heeled shoes
and keeps us in order. We crowd in the kitchen
at the oven smell of shortbread or perhaps
macaroons. We live in that kitchen
and stuff ourselves with home-made sweets
patty cakes and stale cornflakes
made into crumbly nibbles. It is magic.
She despairs over sponges
but the icing tricks us into almost anything.
At our Grandma's house we are allowed
slivers of frothy spongecake, a treat
the adults nod over. The pecking order is maintained
though no one's kitchen is the same as Mum's.

4.

In ninety years she made her investment in family
and at last the harvest is brought in. The years
have been walled up in her eyes. She learned
not to expect too much. Droughts and floods
are our lot and in the good seasons
she tended her garden.
Her long-standing joy was the fernery
and on hot evenings she would stand with the hose
long after we were all squatting around the radio.
It is only now that I remember things she valued
other than family, all those clamorous selves.

5.

Childhood was buttons and pushing them into tight holes
so that your braces could hold up your pants
so that your fly would hold in your dick
(we did not wear underpants until puberty);
in winter, even my slippers had buttons
and she knelt down to fix them. By the time
we could do that ourselves, our slippers
were Turkish design, like Dad's.

My mother kept bottles filled with buttons
cut off old shirts and men's trousers
and the few coloured and varied ones
from old dresses. Those were ghosts of the '20s
and time's unbelievable frivolity.
I did not believe my mother had ever owned up
to using them on a shimmery gown or some party dress.
After the War my mother's button jars
filled with mother-of-pearl and the first plastics.
We were into the age of zips.

My mother had green eyes. "When I was a girl
I was lithe as a cat". But we could hardly believe
those old photos. Now, in her final shape
it is not an old child but a captive
trapped in shrinkage and silence.
The eyes that hold onto me are asking
that the debt be repaid. The only good currency
is to be there, perhaps to hold her nerveless hand.
In these last years she never, once,
referred to our father.

7.

The queen of the kitchen threw off her apron
like that. "I'm going to the Retirement Home
and I'll never have to cook again." The Early Kooka
stove had been our altar, not hers. It gleamed
and was never greasy. The frying pans were scrubbed
and the steel wool scoured her fingers and, later, ours.
We counted ourselves well off.
At some stage a gas hot-water system
with its pilot flame gave point to our western wall.
We would climb onto a chair to peek through the hole
in the cream enamel. "It's still on, it's still on"
we would exclaim if Mum caught us.

We grew in that kitchen, underfoot, under the table,
unbalancing the uka-ants, playing tanks and submarines,
opening cupboard doors, helping stack the groceries,
reciting our homework, eating our Saos and vegemite,
asking what's for tea. No other room belonged to us
so fully. Once, when she was in hospital,
it became a shell,
and we moved as carefully and strangely
as if it were our Grandma's tidy kitchen.
How could we believe, in all those years,
she was serving time?

8.

We define our mother in childhood
needing to take her for granted.
That is our greatest tribute:
granting her the security of our need,
asking, asking and never conscious of giving.

"I've come, mum. Here are some flowers,
something you can look at. And I'll read to you.
After that, I'll speak of the past, I'll
tell you what I remember. The things that come back—
your tennis club and you all in white,
all the neighbours who came over with sick babies
for your advice, you were the sage of young mothers.
Or the Time Of The Naughty Storm, the year
of the sunburn, the marshmallow that failed that time
and smelled of the abattoir." Does she smile?
It is my voice that smiles. It tries hard.
All my stories return to her kitchen.
It is twenty-five years since she was busy in there
and we were her real icons, slippery and unpredictable
—or perhaps predictable entirely?

9.

My mother died at ninety. In her last year
she could not speak or move but her eyes
were so important the mashy food we spooned in
might have been that last Banquet with the family
at my brother's birthday the year before.
I remember the pleasure she found in each mouthfull
and the second glass of wine. One sturdy grandson
helped her to her wheelchair. Her hair was thinner
and my own skull shape stared through her humble smile.
In the last year there was no place for smiles.
When I visited from interstate I talked of events,
what I was doing, where the children were.

Now death has converted all to retrospect
my mother returns into that forties kitchen
with corsets on and a floral dress
and one discoloured tooth and a plumpness
that satisfies the need for reassurance
that the good years will fill us out forever,
and we come racing in from school
and yell out "Mum! Mum! I'm home.
Are there any bikkies in the tin?"
Though she was taken so utterly for granted then
something took: the image is clearer than any snapshot
—it moves, and the vividness takes my breath,
superimposing a warm kitchen face
on all but those frightened, final eyes.
This poem records my need, not hers.
My mother died at ninety. In her last year
her eyes were so eloquent
there was no place for smiles.
All those meals: the tribute
that must be gathered out of all those meals.
Weak tea and ordinary biscuits
have become ironic hosts. Like the old kitchen
nothing survives but this curious tribute.
My mother's eyes reduce them all
to a proper irrelevance,

an improper testament. She knows where she is.
It is the present. When will it be over?